Books in Easy English
Stage 2

UFOs

Lewis Jones

Longman

D1719655

Longman Group Limited
London

*Associated companies, branches and
representatives throughout the world*

© Longman Group Ltd 1978

First published 1978

ISBN 0 582 53149 7

Printed in Hong Kong by
Dai Nippon Printing Co (H.K.) Ltd

Acknowledgements

We are grateful to the following tor permission to reproduce copyright
photographs: Camera Press Ltd., for pages 30–31 top (Grathe Sandberg), 38
top right & 40 bottom (Alfred Gescheidt); DPRG UFO Photo Archives, Essex,
England for pages 22, 30 bottom, 33 top, 37 bottom right, 39 left; Photograph
on page 29 from 'Flying Saucers Have Landed', by George Adamski (deceased)
& Desmond Leslie, published in 1953; Keystone Press Agency Ltd., for pages 4,
37 top, 38 bottom; NASA for page 33 bottom.

We regret that we have been unable to trace the copyright holders of the
photographs on pages 37 middle, 38 top left, 39 right, 40 top, 44 & 45, and
would welcome any information that would enable us to do so.

Contents

Fig. 1

4

Saucers in the sky

On June 24, 1947, Kenneth Arnold was flying his plane above the Cascade Mountains of Washington, in the United States. He owned a company that sold things for fire-fighting, and he used his plane for carrying them.

At three o'clock in the afternoon he was near Mount Rainier. A plane was lost in the area, so Arnold flew round for a time and looked for it. He was looking down at the ground, when he noticed some lights away to his left.

There were nine of them in a line: the front one was highest, and the one at the back was lowest. Each object was round and shining, and almost as big as a plane. The objects all travelled in line together, and sometimes they flew in and out among the mountains. Once, they passed behind one of the mountain-tops.

Arnold noticed where they were at different times, and wrote it down. One question that interested him was: How fast were the objects flying? When he landed, he looked at his notes: 75 kilometres in 102 seconds. That meant the objects were travelling at 2700 kilometres an hour. That's what he told the newspapers later.

The newspapermen asked him: 'How were these objects moving?'

'Each one moved up and down as it travelled,' he said, 'like a saucer when you throw it along the top of the water.'

This answer was taken up by most of his listeners. And next day newspapers all over the United States said Kenneth Arnold saw 'flying saucers' over the Cascade Mountains.

Arnold didn't say that at all. He talked of objects that *moved like* saucers thrown across water. He didn't say they *looked like* saucers. But it was too late to make changes. Flying saucers were in the news.

Questions with no answers

A few days later, in Nevada, someone else in a plane saw five or six round objects, away to his right. That same night, four Air Force officers in Alabama saw a strange light in the sky. As it travelled, it sometimes turned left, sometimes right. Sometimes it moved very fast, sometimes slower.

A woman saw ten of them shoot across the sky above her house. A driver in Iowa saw thirteen of them. In New Mexico several people in a car watched a strange light cross the whole sky in thirty seconds. In Chicago a woman saw one 'with legs'.

A policeman in Portland, Oregon, looked up one day and saw five large objects like saucers. They were travelling very fast, and they seemed to be turning round and round as they went. A few minutes later, two other policemen noticed three of the same objects. Then some of the other people in Portland began to see them.

That night, the crew of a plane in Idaho saw five 'some-things'.

One morning, five Air Force men were sitting in a truck when four of them saw an unusual object in the sky. There were two pieces on top that seemed to turn slowly. The object made no sound. After about 90 seconds, the men lost it.

All this—and more—less than two weeks after Arnold's story.

When United States Air Force planes began to find their way into newspaper stories, the Air Force became troubled. It wasn't answering any more questions from newspapers: it just stopped talking. This made people feel uneasy.

Why was the Air Force saying nothing? What did it know? Why was it hiding things? Was the truth too fearful to tell?

Visitors from another world?

Maybe this uneasiness caused even more trouble. People began *trying* to see flying saucers. More people began looking at the sky. They saw things they hadn't noticed before. Anything unusual *may* be a strange flying object, so more people telephoned their newspaper—and there were more flying saucer stories. And the Air Force were still not talking.

It's useful to understand their reasons. There had been other stories of strange flying objects since the war. More than a thousand of these stories came from Sweden in 1946 alone. Some people thought those objects were Russian—Sweden was a long way from the United States.

But here was something quite different—now unkown objects were flying across the United States itself.

'What's happening?' people wanted to know 'Do these objects come from Russia? Are they *safe*?'

At that time, Russia and the United States were not at all friendly. The Russians were building many new planes that could reach the USA. Maybe they had new bombs as well.

The USA was planning to send its U-2 plane high over Russian skies. Maybe the flying objects were Russian, doing the same kind of thing in the USA—looking, watching, learning. Perhaps an enemy was bringing a new kind of war to the skies over the USA. Were Kenneth Arnold's flying saucers part of that war?

These were the questions that troubled the United States government. It's not surprising that the Air Force stopped talking to newspapers.

But people were still asking questions. Kenneth Arnold (among others) was happy to give them answers. Like the newspapers, he too was soon talking of saucers that flew. He wrote a small book of fifteen pages—The Flying Saucer as

I saw it. And to the question 'Where do they come from?' he had a clear answer: 'From another world.'

A newspaperman who wrote about a saucer (Arnold said) died of unknown causes. A plane hit Mount Rainier, and everyone in the plane was killed. This was *before* Arnold saw his flying objects, but still (he said) this had something to do with the saucers.

A bridge in Idaho was strangely set on fire by 'something'. One saucer was able to get away because it knew the *thoughts* of the man who flew after it.

When the Air Force was asked, 'Is all this true?' they still had nothing to say. And that only made things worse.

People thought: 'If all these stories are untrue, the government will just say so. But they're not saying anything. Why not? The stories must be true.'

So there was the answer at last. Arnold must be right. The flying saucers must be visitors from another world.

What killed Captain Mantell?

'Do you believe in flying saucers?' At first, this meant, 'Do you believe Kenneth Arnold?' Then—when other people saw unusual things—it meant, 'Are these things truly there in the sky? Or only in people's minds?'

But soon it meant something different: 'Do you believe these objects come from another world?'

The *believers* answered, 'Yes. We do have visitors, and they are not from our world.'

The *non-believers* answered, 'No. There must be some other cause.'

The believers couldn't give good reasons, and the non-believers couldn't think of good causes. But the believers seemed more sure of themselves—they certainly made the most noise. It was mostly the believers who telephoned the newspapers and wrote the books. But their story needed another chapter—an interesting one, something surprising.

A few months after Arnold's flight, they got one. It happened at an airport in Kentucky, on January 7, 1948.

That afternoon the airport got a telephone call from the police. Several people were phoning the police about a strange flying object.

'Can you identify it?' the police asked.

The airport said there were no flights in the area.

About twenty minutes later, the police called again. This time, people from two other towns were seeing the object. They said it was round, about 90 metres across, and moving quite fast. The airport made some phone calls of its own, then called the police.

'There are no planes in the area from *any* airport,' they said. 'There's nothing.'

Then the people at the airport itself saw it. Several officers looked at it long and carefully through field-glasses, but they couldn't identify it. At half-past two, everyone was wondering what to do about it, when four fighter-planes came towards the airport.

The pilot of one of the planes was Captain Thomas Mantell. The airport called him on the radio. They asked him to take a look at the object, and try to identify it. One of the four pilots hadn't much fuel left, so he flew on to his own airport. The other two pilots stayed with Mantell, and the three planes began to look for the object.

At first the three pilots could see nothing, and the airport had to help them. Mantell went up to 3000 metres, and left the other two pilots behind. At 2.45 he called the airport and said, 'I see something above me. I'm going up.'

One of the other two pilots asked the airport, 'What are we looking for?'

The airport called Mantell: 'Can you identify the object?'

'It's still above me,' he called back. 'But I'm getting closer. I'm going up to 6000 metres.'

By now Mantell was far above the other two pilots, and they lost him. They called him on the radio, but they got no answer. They thought he must be in trouble. But they couldn't find him, and soon they hadn't much fuel left, so they had to return to their own airport. When they landed, one pilot refuelled and flew back again. He flew all round the area, but he didn't see Mantell, and he didn't see the object. At 3.50 the airport lost the object.

A few minutes later they had some news. Mantell was dead. His plane crashed into the ground and he was killed at once. No one knew why it crashed.

But the believers knew why Mantell was dead. He fought with a flying saucer and lost. And with a dead pilot, of course the plane crashed.

The believers' story had its surprising new chapter—an Air Force pilot was killed by something (someone?) from another world.

A new word comes into English

Questions rained hard and fast on to the US Air Force. How did Mantell die? What happened to his plane? And of course—what was the Air Force hiding?

The Air Force weren't hiding anything: they were busy trying to find the truth themselves, and it all took time. In the months that followed, reports began to come in from other countries. In Norway and Denmark and Sweden and Germany, people were reporting 'balls of fire travelling slowly across the sky.' The reports were unclear, and most of them were from newspapers. Soon there were reports from all over Europe and South America.

In the USA, the Air Force was having word trouble.

'Flying saucer' was changing its meaning. At first it meant 'something unusual in the sky'. Now it meant 'something from another world'. And not all reports spoke of things in the form of a saucer. The Air Force didn't want to talk of flying saucers any more. So they made up a new name— Unidentified Flying Object.

Almost at once it became known by its first letters: UFO.

A UFO could be *anything*. But not everyone was happy with the new name. If something is only in a man's mind, ought you to call it an *object*? If it isn't moving in the sky, or if it's only a light, can you say it's *flying*? Suppose you can't *identify* it, but someone else can. It's a UFO for you, but not for him.

'Unidentified' means *hasn't* been identified. (It may be identified later.) But surely we're talking about something quite different: things that *can't* be identified—by anyone. If you can identify my Unidentified Flying Object, isn't it then an Identified Flying Object? Has my UFO become your IFO?

Today it's best not to think of the three letters or the three words. UFO is just one word, and it's new. Today it means *the cause of a report*. The report may be wrong. The thing may be in someone's mind, or it may be a true object. Maybe it's flying and maybe it isn't. It may be in the sky, or it may be on the ground (and someone believes it has just landed). Maybe some people can identify it and some can't.

None of this matters. As soon as someone *reports* it, it becomes a UFO. Today, the word tells you that someone has made a report—nothing more, nothing less.

But in 1948, the US Air Force was not only in word trouble. It didn't know that 1948 would bring the third of the great UFO reports.

Three great UFOs

At 8.30 in the evening on October 1, a plane was coming in to an airport in North Dakota. The pilot was 25-year-old George Gorman. He flew round the airport for a time, and about nine o'clock he called the airport on his radio. He said he wanted to land. The airport told him there was a small plane (a Piper Cub) in the area. Gorman saw the Cub.

Then he called the airport again. 'The light of another plane has just passed me on my right. Why didn't you tell me?'

The airport said there were no planes in the area except the Cub. Gorman could still see the light, so he turned and went after it. He could see the form of the Cub against the city lights under him, but he could see no form of a plane near the strange light.

He went faster, until he was a thousand metres from the light. It was about 20 cm across, and it was going on-off-on-off. Then it stayed on, and moved away fast. It turned left and crossed over the airport buildings. Then it went up very fast and Gorman followed it.

At 2000 metres up, it turned again, and came towards Gorman's plane. He thought the UFO was trying to hit him, and he had to drop quickly out of the way. It missed him by a metre or two. Once again both Gorman and the UFO turned and came towards each other, and once again Gorman had to pull his plane away. Then the UFO went up very fast and was lost.

'The thing seemed to be *thinking*,' Gorman said later.

The Air Force asked for reports from other people. There were two people in the Piper Cub—the pilot and another man. Both of them saw a light that moved fast. But they didn't see all the turnings of Gorman's plane. Two people on the ground saw a light move over the field once.

By that time there was a team of Air Force officers with just one job—studying UFOs. Men from this team now moved fast—they came at once to the airport. If UFOs are from another world (some people think) perhaps they make things radio-active. (But why? No one gave any reasons.) Was Gorman's plane radio-active? The Air Force team wanted to find out.

Before they came, they asked the airport to keep the plane on the ground. They wanted to see it before it flew again. The team reached the airport in only a few hours. They studied the plane most carefully from top to bottom, from front to back. Then they asked to see another plane: 'one that hasn't flown for a few days'.

Before they left, they were able to bring one new piece to the story—Gorman's plane was more radio-active.

The Air Force now had the three great UFOs on its books: Arnold—Mantell—Gorman. These three names are well known to every believer. By the end of 1948 the UFO team had hundreds of other reports. Most of these UFOs were soon identified. But a few—about 30 or 40—were still marked 'unknown'.

The US Air Force—like everyone else—wanted to answer the question: 'What are UFOs?' And the Air Force team was asked to write a report. They did. Their answer was: 'UFOs must come from another world.'

When the report made its way up to General Vandenberg, it was sent back down again. And some months later, that report was burnt. Again, some people said the Air Force were trying to hide the truth. The truth is that the report's reasons for its answer were not good enough. The report began with 'We have not met anything like this before...' And jumped at once to 'So it cannot come from our own world.'

Then and later, a number of the Air Force team believed

in visitors from 'out there'. And they were so sure, that for them *unkown* meant *true UFO*. For them, UFO still had its older meaning: an *object* that was *flying* and was *not identified*.

But when you mark something 'true flying-object', you bring the study of that report to an end. If it *is* from another world, how could we possibly understand it? Is it any use trying?

Happily, not everyone thought the same way. Later, people took out the old reports and read them again. They dug out the 'unknowns' and took a long, hard look at them. They looked for holes in the picture, for new ways to discover the truth, for people to talk to, for new questions to ask.

And they found them.

Some answers

In 1952 the man in change of the Air Force UFO team was Edward Ruppelt. One day he got a phone call from Washington: a lot of people were still asking questions about the Mantell UFO, and there seemed to be a lot of different answers. Just what *was* the answer?

Ruppelt began digging. He sent for the Mantell report and read it very carefully. Mantell said on his radio, 'I'm going up to 6000 metres.' They were the last words he spoke.

At 6000 metres it's unsafe for a pilot who isn't carrying oxygen. There isn't enough air: without oxygen no one can stay awake. Mantell wasn't carrying oxygen. Every pilot was told again and again: 'DO NOT go above 4500 metres without oxygen. Not at ANY time. EVER.' The pilots of the two other planes followed this order: they stayed at 4500 metres. Mantell went up much higher.

No one knows why. He said he was getting closer to the

UFO. Perhaps he was so keen on reaching it that he wasn't thinking about oxygen. Maybe he thought he could safely get up and down again quickly. Instead, he ran into oxygen trouble, and his plane dropped out of the sky. It came down so fast that pieces broke off before it hit the ground.

So Mantell didn't die a strange death: he died because you can't pilot a plane if you're not awake. But that still left the question: What was the UFO? Mantell was going after *something* for 15 or 20 minutes. Ruppelt read through the rest of the report.

Not long after the UFO was lost, a man phoned the Air Force. He saw an object crossing the sky. He looked at it through a telescope—and it was a balloon. At 4.45 someone in Tennessee phoned. He also saw something travelling across the sky, and he also had a telescope. He looked through his telescope and identified the object—a balloon.

A balloon? Surely a pilot like Mantell would know a balloon? But Ruppelt sent for reports of winds that day, and in a few days he had them. He was able to fix a possible course for a balloon in those winds. It was just about right for the reports from different towns.

But nobody that day said they saw a balloon. What *did* they say about the UFO? Ruppelt looked again at the reports: '...round...round...round...'

It left only one question: Why didn't Mantell know it was a balloon?

In 1947 a new kind of balloon took to the skies. It was not like the balloons that pilots knew. It was very big—30 metres across—the kind they called a 'skyhook'. From the ground you could see a skyhook balloon at 18,000 metres —18 kilometres up in the sky. Mantell didn't know about them because almost *no one* knew about them. At that time, skyhooks were a secret.

So here was *one* UFO that wasn't from another world.

And Gorman? His plane was radio-active. But they soon discovered that this isn't unusual. A plane that has just been flying is always more radio-active than a plane on the ground. It becomes more radio-active when it flies above 6000 metres. And the UFO? Gorman fought a *lighted* balloon. The Air Force reports are very clear about it.

Kenneth Arnold? No one can be sure now. But the sky-hooks first went up in that same year—1947. And often a few smaller balloons were used instead of one big one. But it's too long ago now—Arnold's flying saucers have to stay 'unknown'.

Balloons are not a secret any more now. But they can still surprise people who see them for the first time. About a hundred-thousand of the smaller ones are sent up every year in the USA alone. Many balloons are more than a hundred metres across: they're mostly used to study the sky, and they may carry a 3000-kilogram telescope.

At night big balloons often carry lights. In the daytime, if dark objects are carried under the balloon, they can look like a hole in the middle of the round form.

Winds high in the sky can be very different from winds on the ground, and they can travel at hundreds of kilo-metres an hour. Sometimes the big skyhooks were lost, but the Air Force discovered an easy way to find them again—they followed the balloon's course by reading the reports of flying saucers.

In 1964 a big balloon was sent up in Arizona, and it went as high as 42 kilometres. It started a number of UFO reports. The people of a small town in Virginia came out with their guns. The police tried to stop them, but they couldn't. The men went together to a field, to catch the little green men. Happily, they didn't find them.

'Is this report true?'

The early Air Force studies of UFOs were rather poor. Often, their officers didn't know the best way to get at the truth. Their job was to answer questions about the unusual in the sky, but often they didn't fully understand even the usual.

The Air Force was sometimes afraid of what they heard, and reports were kept secret. Several of the UFO team were believers, and wanted to show that we had visitors from another world. And still the Air Force left the work in the hands of these people.

They seemed to ask themselves, 'Do we have any reason to *disbelieve* this report?' But in these areas of study, you must be slow to believe. We ought to ask ourselves, 'Can we sure about this? Are we certain? Is this report clearly true? Is it trouble-free? *Must* it be true? Can we safely believe this man? Is he being truthful? Have we any reason to *believe* this report?'

A men tells you he's seen a flying object. It travels, he says, at thousands of kilometres an hour. It can stop and fly at once towards a different part of the sky. It can turn and change course in surprising ways. It can stay at one place in the sky. A second later, it may not be there at all. And during all this, it makes no sound.

Now these things seem to be impossible, and you know that. What are you going to do? Throw out all you know, so that this one report can be true? You've seen, perhaps, a thousand flying objects that *can't* do these things. And here is *one* that (perhaps) can. Do you throw away the thousand and keep the one? Were you wrong about every one of the thousand? Perhaps you were.

But notice something else. You're not throwing away your thousand old objects and getting one good new one.

17

All you're getting is a *report*. The Air Force was often wrong about this. They often thought they were studying something in the sky. But they were not. They were only studying reports.

The US Air Force asked Professor Donald Menzel to study the UFO team itself. He did, and he was not happy.

UFOs in a man's eye

The team often believed people who just didn't know enough. When a man saw something and said, 'It couldn't be a plane,' the Air Force believed him.

At these times, Professor Menzel said, the UFO team ought to ask two questions. First: 'You know that many things in the sky are not unusual: which of these things was your UFO most like?' And when he answers, ask him the second question: 'Why do you think your UFO is not one of those?'

Menzel found that people often said, 'It couldn't be a plane, *because I couldn't hear it*.' Or, at night, 'I know it wasn't a plane because its light was too strong.' Asking both these questions is very useful, Menzel said. 'Right now, if a man says a UFO wasn't a plane, you believe him. And you write down NOT A PLANE. If you ask my two questions, you learn something helpful: this man doesn't know enough about planes—he thinks you can always hear them. And then you do *not* write NOT A PLANE.'

But the Air Force never used Menzel's two questions.

The UFO team always asked, 'Were you wearing glasses when you saw the UFO?' Sometimes of course the answer was no, and the Air Force asked nothing more about it. Menzel wanted them to ask, 'Do you *usually* wear glasses? *Ought* you to wear them? When did a doctor last look at your eyes? Is there anything wrong with them?'

The Air Force wouldn't use these questions, or most of Menzel's other questions.

Menzel looked at one of the team's reports. A child got out of bed in the middle of the night. He turned on the light, which woke his father. Then the light went out again. The father looked out of the window, and saw a light in the sky. It was rather red. It moved about in the sky for a short time, then it became less strong, and soon it wasn't there. A UFO.

When you're in a dark room, said Menzel, and a strong light comes on and goes off again, it leaves its picture in your eye. This is an after-image. When you move your eye, the after-image moves with it. If you look at the night sky, you'll see the after-image moving against the sky. Here was a UFO that wasn't in the sky at all—it was inside a man's eye.

With an after-image, the usual questions are a waste of time. (How far away was it? What was it made of? How fast was it moving?) But the Air Force team's questions were all like that: there was no way of identifying an after-image.

It's not surprising, said Menzel, that the Air Force finds so many 'unknowns'. If you think an after-image is a UFO, it will seem to move very fast. When you begin to lose the image, the 'UFO' will seem to become smaller, and travel away from you. The colours can change as you watch it. If you look at the light for only a short time, the after-image will also last only a short time: your UFO will seem to come and go very quickly.

Menzel took out another of the Air Force reports. A man in Oregon watched a point of light moving in the night sky. Menzel thought it seemed like a satellite. And there *was* a satellite going round the world at that time. But the report said the UFO could not be a satellite for two reasons. The satellite was too close to the skyline that night—no one could see it. And the man said the light moved fast-slow-fast-stop-fast. Menzel spent some time on the report. At last he found that the date was wrong: the object *was* a satellite. And the stop-go course came, not from the satellite itself, but from the man's eye.

When you're looking at something, your eye is never at rest. It moves a little all the time. And if you're watching something very small, the object often seems to move instead.

Another report marked 'unknown' came from Ohio. A woman was driving a car with the top down, when she noticed a light in the sky above. It seemed to be turning. Every time she stopped the car, the UFO stopped: when she started again, the UFO followed. She was afraid, and drove home quickly.

At first she thought it could be the moon, but it moved a little up and down all the time. Menzel says she was right the first time: it was the moon. It was not a very clear sky, and the moon was in the right place. If you look at a small light in a dark room—and there's nothing else near it—the light will seem to move about. There's nothing unusual about this—it happens to everyone. And again it's the moving eye that causes it. (And of course the moon always seems to stop and start with a moving car.)

The Air Force asked Menzel to look at more of their UFO reports over the years. They usually sent him 'unknowns'. Menzel studied them, and changed most of them to 'knowns'.

'What are they hiding?'

In January 1953 the US government (secretly!) brought together a new team of people, and gave them 75 of the 'best' UFO reports from the past two years.

They asked the team: 'Do we seem to have visitors from another world?'

The new team studied the reports and said no. But this team's report was also kept secret, and stayed secret for more than thirteen years. And again, people believed there must be something to hide.

Philip Klass was a newspaperman in Washington. He says: 'People always believe the government can "hide the truth". It can't. For the USA, 1962 was a time of deep trouble with Cuba and the Russians. President Kennedy kept his plans highly secret in the ten days before 22 October. Only very few people knew what was happening.'

But several newspapers soon knew the truth—and kept it to themselves.

Few secrets can be kept from Washington newspapermen. Visits from other worlds would be perhaps the biggest news story of all time. It's impossible for thousands of government people to hide that kind of thing for even a month. Certainly not for ten years.

Some knowns

It was becoming clear that the sky itself was very new to most people. They spent a lifetime looking down, and looking around. Then came all the talk of strange things in the sky. And they looked up—and began to see them. The sky is full of things, and many people have never seen them before. It's quite easy to find something you don't understand at first.

Menzel himself told of a UFO he saw in 1955. He was flying in the Arctic when he saw something come very fast from the skyline towards the plane. Green and red lights went off and on. It stopped at once about a hundred metres away. It moved quickly to one side, flew away past the

Fig. 2   Fig. 3

The sky is full of strange things. What do you think these are?

skyline and was lost, then came back again. And then—at last—he knew what it was: the star Sirius.

A star is only a point of light, and it may seem strange that it could look like a UFO. And to the eye, stars don't move. How could one of them seem to shoot about the sky like this? Down near the skyline, stars can seem to move in surprising ways. When a strong light is near the skyline, you look at it through a great deal of air. And air moves and changes like the waters of the sea. When the night is clear, the air often breaks up white light into different colours. When you haven't seen this before, it can be hard to believe. Stars are Menzel's life work, but he too was at first surprised.

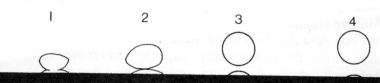

Fig. 4

When the sun rises or sets you can sometimes see strange shapes in the sky. A seaman on a boat in the English Channel saw two suns (as in the picture). One was rising and the other was setting.

22

Professor Carl Sagan's life work is about other worlds: the other eight planets that go round our sun, and also the planets that go round other suns. He's helping with the plans to look for life, on Mars and other planets.

'I was once giving a talk,' he said. 'And at the end, there were some questions about UFOs. I said they seemed mostly to be unsurprising things to me. They seemed strange to someone who didn't understand them. They seemed unusual to someone who saw them for the first time. As I left at the end, two policemen outside were pointing up at the sky. I looked up and I saw a strange, very strong light: it was moving slowly. Of course I went away quickly, before people could ask me what it was.'

He went out to eat with some friends, and he took them outside and pointed to the sky. 'At times the light was bright and strong, and sometimes it was harder to see. And there was no sound. Well, I went home and got my field-glasses. When I looked through them I was able to make out the lights. The bright white light was *two* lights close together. There were two lights at each side, and they were going on and off. When the thing got brighter, we could hear a quiet, low sound; when the thing lost its brightness, we couldn't hear a thing. It was a plane.'

Afterwards, Sagan said, 'No one was very pleased about that—it doesn't make a very good story if you go home and say, "You know what happened? We went out to eat, and there was a bright light outside, and it was a plane." Nobody's interested. But *just suppose*. Suppose no one had any field-glasses. Then the story goes: "There was this great light out there and it was moving around the city, and we don't know anything about it. *Maybe it's visitors from another planet*." Now that's a better story, and people will listen to it. They just like to hear about surprising things, and visitors from another planet are certainly a surprise.'

The best-known UFO of all

Arthur C Clarke has been writing about planets and satellites all his life. Long before he wrote *2001* for the cinema, he said, 'I don't believe in UFOs. The reason is—I've seen too many. Anybody can see them, during the course of a few years, if he takes the trouble to look at the sky at all. What I want to say is this. The sky holds endless kinds of things to see. Any one person may see only a few a lifetime. But if he looks, he will surely see one of them. When he doesn't understand them, he may think they're surprising and very wonderful—not just new to him.'

During the war, in 1942, Clarke was working in Britain. 'On a quiet summer day,' he says, 'I saw the loveliest of all my UFOs. I looked carefully, and I could just see the moon: it looked lost and alone in the clear daylight sky. And beside it was a bright white point of light. It shone like a star —where no star ought to be. It was very bright—much brighter than the moon. It was close to the moon's edge, and it didn't seem to move. But after I watched it for about ten minutes, I noticed that it was moving slowly towards the moon—until at last, after about an hour, it reached the edge. It seemed to become part of the moon.'

Clarke had a telescope. 'The war had to wait as we all had a good look. I don't think we'll ever forget it. I said it shone where no star ought to be, and this was right—no star is bright enough to shine in the daylight sky. But there is one *planet* that is bright enough—you can see the planet Venus for most of the year, even in the daytime, if you know where to look for her.'

Clarke was pleased by his UFO, but he was not surprised. 'Through hundreds of years,' he says, 'people have noticed her in daylight and sent up shouts of wonder. But she has been there all the time, just like the moon. A surprising number of people don't even know the *moon* can be seen in the daytime sky. That summer afternoon, Venus passed *behind* the moon, and was hidden. About an hour later, it came out at the other side, and shone as brightly as before.'

There are people who say, 'Men like these know *about* the sky. But they don't live in it and work in it. A pilot does. The pilot of a plane would identify these things at once: the sky is his world.'

Edward Ruppelt (later in charge of the US Air Force's UFO team) was a pilot during World War II. 'One night,' he says, 'just after we dropped our bombs, a night-fighter came at us very fast. Part of the back of the plane was red-hot—every one saw it as he shot towards us. I fired with all six guns. I'm glad I missed: the "night-fighter" was Venus.' Ruppelt was firing at something 40 million kilometres away.

In the UFO reports, Venus is perhaps the cause more often than anything else. In Britain during World War II, there were always more UFO reports when Venus was in the night sky.

In the USA in 1967, a man reported a UFO. It landed several times a week, between about 4.30 and 7.30 in the evening. It was between 10 and 30 kilometres away, its colour was green, and it was as big as a house. Sometimes he saw two lines of windows, and the object seemed to have jet engines under it. These engines helped to light up the countryside near it. It always came down very slowly, and when it landed, it cut off its lights.

O	red O	green	green
orange	O	O	O

Fig. 5

A seaman on a boat in the Indian Ocean on Dec 6, 1957 saw the planet Venus. The planet changed colour as it was setting and for a few moments he also saw two planets.

25

When someone from a UFO team came to see the man, he was still watching the object through field-glasses. The UFO was Venus.

In that same year, another UFO was reported, but this time by many people—police officers in eleven different towns were busy with this UFO for four days. At 4.36 in the evening of Day 1, some policemen saw a light like a bright red football. When they got closer, it moved away, and they followed it for about 12 kilometres out into the country. It seemed to be about as big as the moon in the sky. They lost it and went back to town, but the UFO was following them.

'It lit the inside of the police car, so we could read our watches. We radioed that a flying object was following us. When we stopped the car, it turned away and we lost it behind some trees.'

The object moved higher into the sky above the trees, and its colour changed from red to a bright white. Then it took the form of a large plant with four parts. When the car went back into town, the object began to move very fast.

On Day 2 the object followed a man along the road.

On Day 3 a plane went up, and the police turned on their car lights to show the pilot the UFO. The pilot saw the UFO above him, and began to chase it.

'When we flew towards it, it backed off. It got smaller, until it was as small as the end of a pencil. We went to about a thousand metres, but it still moved higher and away from us. The colour was an unchanging white.'

On the ground, a police car was chasing a ball of light just outside town: it was just above the trees, and travelling at 120 kilometres an hour. Another policeman reported that a dark-blue ball was chasing *him*. And two policemen reported a red-and-white ball 8 metres across. Red and green and white lights were going on and off, and it was moving away from their town.

It's hard to believe that all these reports were of the same thing, but it's true. Every day, this UFO went slowly higher in the sky, and 'became like a star'. It wasn't a star, but an old friend of the UFO team—the planet Venus.

How can so many people be wrong?

How big? How far? How fast?

One of the troubles is this. People are often asked: 'How far away was it?' and usually they will tell you. (They almost *never* say, 'I don't know.') But they ought to answer a second question: 'How do you know?' or 'Why do you think that?' This second question ought also to follow answers to: 'How big was it?' and 'How fast was it travelling?'

Suppose you see something travel across the sky, over your head, and it takes ten seconds. You may think like this: the skyline is about five kilometres away on each side of me. So this UFO travelled 10 kilometres in 10 seconds. That is, one kilometre a second—which is 60 kilometres a minute. A speed of 3600 km an hour. It's even faster than Kenneth Arnold's flying saucers.

We'll suppose that your ten seconds was right. But what about those ten kilometres? How do you know this object went from skyline to skyline? You noticed it at one side of you, it travelled above you, and you lost it at the other side. Maybe it only travelled a few metres, like a paper plane. Something that passes just above your head can seem to move fast. But if it's high in the sky—*at the same speed*—your eye will see it moving very slowly.

You need to know how high an object is. If you don't know that, you can't tell its speed—*nobody can*. If the object is something you know, *then* you may know how far away it is. Suppose you've seen a Concorde plane before. If you now watch one going higher in the sky, it will become smaller. This helps you to know how far away it is.

Kenneth Arnold said his saucers were at a distance of 40 km. But how did he know? He thought they were small enough to be at that distance. But how did he know? They were about 15 metres across, he said. But how did he know *that*? He didn't. Arnold couldn't know how big the saucers were, or their distance, or their speed. So his numbers are not much help.

Many people began taking a long hard look at UFO reports: they didn't believe everything they were told any more. But still the unknowns kept coming. Unhappily, it's very easy to make an unknown.

Suppose I tell you a UFO came down in my back garden yesterday: and little green men got out and talked to me. What are you going to do about it? It's not there now, so there's nothing to see—you can't go back to yesterday. You may not believe me, but you don't *know* what happened, do you? Most of my report may be untrue, but maybe *some* of it is true. How are you going to find out? You can't, of course, so you have to mark my report 'unknown'.

This just means: 'There's no way to find out the truth now.' But some people will think 'unknown' means: 'This couldn't possibly be a plane or Venus or a balloon or any of the more usual things. The UFO wasn't caused by anything in this world. So it must come from some other planet.'

Pictures or words?

In California, George Adamski said he went for rides in a flying saucer, and it took him to a 'mother ship'. He met a lovely girl dressed in gold, who spoke in little musical sounds. As George didn't understand music, they talked to each other with thoughts. Since then, other people have ridden in saucers (they say). None of the visitors seems to have much to say.

But for Adamski, words were not enough. He thought he ought to have pictures too—so he gave us photographs. And what photographs! (fig. 6) When one of his flying saucers landed, there were clearly three suns in the sky (or he photographed the little saucer with light from three lamps).

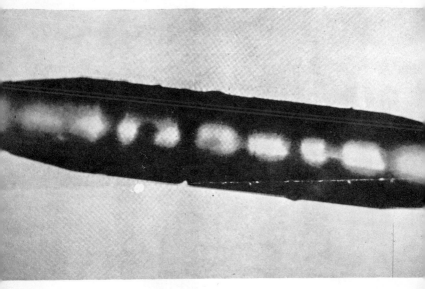

Fig. 6   A UFO's mothership?

Pictures seem the right answers when no one believes what you say. ('They won't believe my words, so now I'll give them something they *must* believe — photographs.') And so, from all the years, and from the hundreds of reports, we now have photographs to study.

We can look at pictures of unclear lights in the sky, footmarks in the ground, fields where a flying saucer has

Fig. 7   Did a UFO land here in Norway?

Fig. 8   Can you identify some of the pictures here?

Fig. 9

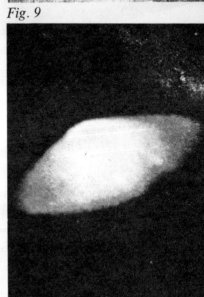

landed—and of course left again. Many pictures of objects look sadly like things you can find in the home. Could the UFO in fig. 8 come from the kitchen? Is a table lamp showing in fig. 9? You may like to try and identify some of the pictures in this book.

At 11.30 on a summer night in 1965, a man in Philadelphia was photographing the moon. Then, he says, a UFO came over the hill behind his home. As usual, the photographs are very unclear—because the UFO was moving quickly, he says (and he himself moved).

He and his brother watched the object for about half a minute, then it moved up into the sky very fast and they lost it. It made no sound.

A year later, the US Air Force asked Dr Edward Condon for a complete Study of Unidentified Flying Objects. Many people helped with the Condon Report: the man who studied all the photographs was William Hartmann.

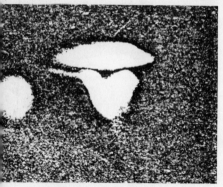

Is this a real UFO or is it a photograph of a plate and a hand?

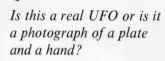

Fig. 11 opposite page ►
Just before light reaches the photographic film, it has to pass through glass. Is this UFO a light on the glass?

Fig. 10a

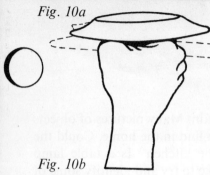

Fig. 10b

Fig. 12a/Fig. 12b ►
Objects in the sky or marks on the film?

He was not surprised by the two photographs from Philadelphia, because the object under the UFO was very like a hand and an arm. (fig. 10a).

Sometimes there's something wrong with the photo-graphic *film*. Even when you don't take a picture at all, the photograph can show strange 'lights' in the sky.

Try fig. 11 and fig. 12a and 12b. UFOs? Objects in the sky or marks on the film?

Just before light reaches the photographic film, it has to pass through glass in the camera. And sometimes that brings surprises to the photographer.

Fig. 11

Fig. 12a   *Fig. 12b*

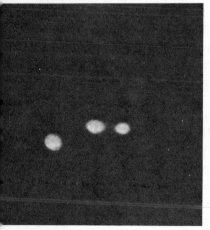

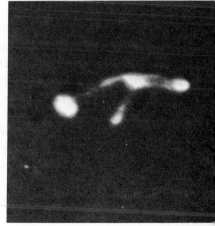

Photographs of what?

William Hartmann says you can believe a man's photograph as much as you can believe his words—no more and no less. People sometimes don't tell the truth, and it's the same with photographs.

If you're studying UFO pictures, a photograph may be very interesting—but what you need is the *film*. Sometimes a man says he took two photographs almost together, one after the other. But the two pictures may be on different parts of the film. He may say he only had time for one quick photograph. But his film could show many photographs (while he tried to get the picture right).

Sometimes, when a UFO picture is brought to a newspaper, they find that the photograph was taken some months before. (Why did the photographer wait so long? What's wrong with his story?)

Sometimes the photographer will say that several photographs were taken in a certain order. But the numbers on the film can show that this is not true.

UFO photographs are studied rather carefully these days, and usually the first question is: 'Show me the film.' This one question can cause a lot of trouble, and photographers know it. So what often happens now is that the film is 'lost'.

But not all UFO pictures are just strange marks on film. Many of them are true photographs—but photographs of what?

The three photographs of fig. 13 were taken by a 13-year-old boy. He was out walking with a friend (he says) when they saw the UFO. The photographic film shows no more than the three photographs. What can you do about pictures like these? You certainly need to study the pictures and the story together. When was the picture taken? Where? What else does the report tell you? How far away

Fig. 13   A boy said that he took these photographs of a UFO.

was the UFO? How big was it? What was it doing when it was photographed?

Professor Frank Drake went and talked to the boy. The photographs were all right for time of year and time of day, and the boy kept his story unchanged for months. His mother and father believed him, his friends believed him. Nothing seemed to be wrong with his report, which was very clear. He answered all of Drake's questions.

The UFO was rather like a saucer. How long? About one metre across. Colour? Shiny all over. Any sound? Yes, a rather high sound that went up and down a little. (His mother heard the same sound the next evening.) Speed? About 30 km an hour. For the second picture, the boy got closer, and for the third picture, he was standing under it. Then it went up and away.

The story seemed all right, and the pictures were still all right. But by this time Professor Drake was not happy about story-and-pictures together. He looked at the boy's camera; it took a photograph very quickly. That is to say, the camera stayed open for a very short time. When a photograph was taken, light came into the camera for less than one per cent of a second. In that time, the UFO (at 30 kph) ought to move about 4 cm. When you photograph something that moves, its picture is not clear. Drake looked again at the third picture. The UFO's edges were clear—too clear for a moving object?

And this moving UFO had to be in different places at different times. But was it? Picture 1 could be the same place as Picture 2. Then Drake looked carefully at the trees in Picture 2. Was the UFO under the same part of the same tree as in Picture 3? Perhaps this object was not moving at all. It was possible, but not certain.

Drake asked the boy to go with him next Saturday, and show him the place. But that night Drake had a phone call. 'The boy was very troubled,' Drake said. 'He knew that when we got to the field, I would see the answer to this UFO —the same tree in all three pictures. So the object didn't move at all.'

The boy made the UFO from paper, and then photographed it on a tree. Even young people can make UFOs quite easily. But with only a photograph to study, it can be very hard to find the truth.

Making UFOs

In April 1966, a man was on a flight to Los Angles when he took (he says) a photograph of a UFO: fig. 15. Have you seen anything like this before?

William Hartmann, working for the Condon Report, was not very interested in this 'UFO'. He himself took a photograph out in the country. And then, *on top of it,* he took a second photograph of a reading-lamp, from one side. Does Hartmann's UFO (fig. 16) tell you anything about the other one?

When an object is near to you in daylight, the light parts are often bright, and the other parts dark. As it moves away into the distance, there's less difference between the light and the dark parts. And bright colours became softer. People who make UFO photographs have sometimes forgotten this. They place a small object close to the camera,

Fig. 14

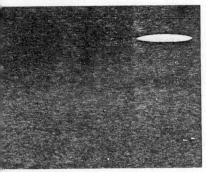

Fig. 15

Fig. 16

Students in Britain made several flying saucers like this, fig. 14. The police and the army looked at them carefully.

Do you think these are real UFOs or holes cut in the photographs? figs. 15 and 16.

You can draw UFOs on glass and then photograph them, fig. 17.

Fig. 17

Fig. 18

Fig. 19

Fig. 20   Many Americans believe that these are flying saucers.

and say that it's a large object far away. What do you think about fig. 18?

An object can seem to be in the air if it's held against glass in front of the camera. Do you think the 'UFO' in fig. 19 is one of these? Sometimes you can see part of the object in the glass itself. Look just to the left of the 'UFO' in fig. 18.

Are the lights in fig. 20 in the sky? This photograph was taken through a window. Suppose there are four lights in the room *behind* the camera. Maybe they are the cause of the UFOs. We don't know the truth now of course (the picture was taken in 1952). But—the lights shining against glass? Possible?

Glass has been useful to many photographers of UFOs. You begin with a photograph (of the sky, or the moon perhaps), and hold some glass above it. You can draw on the glass, or put part of another photograph on it. Then you photograph everything together. How about fig. 21? And fig. 22?

Of course you have to be careful with the light and dark parts. Near Rio de Janeiro in Brazil, in 1952, two newspapermen were out on a job, says their report, when a UFO came towards them at great speed. One of the men

Fig. 21   *Fig. 22*

Can we be sure what these are?

39

was a news photographer: he quickly took up his camera, and took five photographs in about one minute. This has been called one of the best and strongest of all UFO reports.

Dr Donald Menzel studied the photographs and noticed something. The UFO is lighted from the left, but the trees are lighted from the right.

So if you do want to make a UFO picture, take care to get an *unclear* photograph (fig. 23). That could save you a lot of trouble.

It is hard to be sure about one kind of UFO photograph: an object thrown into the air. For fig. 24 and fig. 25,

Perhaps you have seen this before in the kitchen?

Fig. 23

More examples of photographs that people say are real UFOs
Fig. 24

Fig. 25

did someone throw a small object up in the air? And did someone else take a picture with his camera? Or are we seeing visitors from another world?

Do cameras tell the truth?

So the camera can't be an answer to the UFO question. As William Hartmann says in the Condon Report: 'Cameras may tell the truth, but photographers sometimes don't.'

'What's needed for a good report,' he says, 'is not one photographer but several. It's best if they don't know each other, and if they're a long way from each other (tens of kilometres). And their photographs all ought to show the same UFO.' So far, nothing like this has ever happened.

And there are people who say: You must know which object has been photographed, before you can say, 'This is not a flying saucer.'

'There's no need for this at all,' says Hartmann. 'You don't have to say, "This is a fish" before you can say, "This isn't a flower." '

Hartmann finds that nearly all UFO photographs are of four kinds:
1) from untruthful photographers
2) objects that are not unusual (but the photographer couldn't identify them)
3) they're not clear enough to be of any use
4) they come with a report that isn't clear enough.

That leaves less than 5 per cent of unknowns. These unknowns don't become true flying saucers. They don't become anything—that's what 'unknown' means. When you have an unknown, that's not the end of the questions: it's the beginning. And if you can't find any more answers, the unknown is still just that—unknown.

And an unknown can tell you nothing.

But photographs can't show something *happening*. They only catch a little piece out of time—a small part of a second. *Moving pictures* can let you watch for many seconds. They let you see changes. And they can give you 16 different pictures every second.

You can see objects coming closer or moving away. You can study the different pictures in order, and watch an object crossing from side to side. You can learn its speed, and its distance.

It's not unusual for someone to have a camera that takes photographs. But not many people have a movie camera. And when they do, they don't often carry it about with them.

But sometimes, the right three things all come together—a person, a UFO, and a movie-camera.

Pictures that move

At eleven o'clock on a July morning, a man was driving near Tremonton, in Utah, with his wife and two children. The man's wife pointed to some 'bright shining objects in the air'. She couldn't identify them. The man stopped the car and looked. In a clear blue sky, about ten or twelve objects were moving about. The man was a navy photographer, and he had a movie-camera in the car. He took it out and used about nine metres of film. At the end, one of the objects moved away from the others and left them. There was no sound, and the man said there were no planes or birds or balloons near.

The Tremonton film was sent to the US Navy, who studied it carefully. Balloons (they said) usually move together, but these objects were moving about in different ways. Planes would have engines that made a noise. No bird could throw back sunlight as brightly as this. And this was not sunlight from a shiny object—that kind of light seems to go on and off as the object moves about. These objects had their own lights, which shone without changing.

When you watch a film in the cinema, the objects and people seem to move about. But of course the film itself is only a number of photographs. The Tremonton film had 16 photographs every second, and the navy studied these in order.

Each object changed its place a little on different pictures.

'We can suppose,' said the navy, 'that these objects were about 8 km away. An object in one picture has sometimes moved 0.1729 mm in the next picture: this means a speed of 1000 km an hour in the air. At a distance of 16 kilometres, the speed would be 2000 kph.'

In the end, what did the navy think?—'Somebody' was in charge of these objects, and was 'causing' the changes in flight. In other words, these were UFOs from another planet.

William Hartmann studied the Tremonton film again most carefully for the Condon Report. The navy report said the light from the objects was unchanging. But this was not true. The objects did change in brightness. And this is usual when a moving object catches the sunlight. So these objects were not themselves shining. And when an object lost its brightness, it didn't become dark—there was just nothing to see at all. The object was too far away for the eye, or too small. This is just about right for a bird.

And a film, like an eye, sees a very bright object as something too big. Hartmann looked at the film itself: the brightness 'burned right down' into the film, so the objects looked larger on film than they were in the sky.

The navy 'supposed' that the objects were 8 or even 16 km away. Why? There's no reason for these distances. Suppose instead that they were birds. So these objects are only about 20 cm across. And you can see the sunlight on them, but you can't see the birds themselves. This puts them at a distance of perhaps 600 metres. Their speeds would be about 80 kph, which again is about right for birds.

White sea-birds are often seen in that area, and several of them often ride the winds together. Sometimes two or three or four of the filmed objects close together became bright at the same time: birds look just like this when they all turn together. One of the objects left the others—just as a bird often leaves the rest and looks for warmer air to carry it higher.

Figs. 26a and b show some objects moving together: quite usual in birds, but not perhaps in flying saucers.

People sometimes find it hard to believe that birds could look like UFOs. But Hartmann says that he himself was driving near Tremonton shortly after he finished his report. He saw numbers of white sea birds, flying just like the objects in the film. Sometimes in twos, and sometimes alone. Their brightness changed as they moved, and he could see only the light on them, not the birds themselves. (He only knew they *were* birds because he saw them leave the ground.)

Edward Ruppelt (once head of the Air Force UFO team)

Fig. 26a   *Fig. 26b*

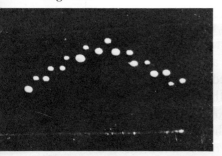 

What are the strange lights?

says that he too watched white sea birds later in San Francisco. They were wheeling around in a clear sky, and they looked just like the UFOs in the Tremonton movie.

Arthur C Clarke looked out of an office window in Australia and saw—flying saucers. It was late afternoon. The sun was low on the skyline, and a line of bright, round objects was moving slowly along above it. They were moving up and down as they went.

Clarke says, 'This was the only time I've ever seen "flying saucers". I've sometimes read about UFOs that were just birds with the sunlight on them. It seemed so stupid that I've never believed it—but it's quite true. I was looking at white sea birds, and their undersides were shining like glass. I've lived beside the sea for many years, and this is the only time

Fig. 27

I've seen anything like it.'

The point is this: even a movie hasn't been able to do better than the eye. The study of 400 pictures on film hasn't

Fig. 28

helped to show a clear difference between flying saucers and birds.

One morning in August 1950, a man took a 30 second film of two white lights moving slowly across the sky (fig. 27). He said they were travelling too fast to be birds.

It's possible that they were planes—perhaps at a greater distance than the planes in fig. 28, so only the brightness was seen. But no one can be sure now. The Condon Report had to mark them 'unknown'.

All movie films of UFOs have shown the same kind of thing—lights in the sky. And after a great deal of study, that is still all we can report—lights in the sky.

A radio eye

But eyes and cameras were not the only things looking for UFOs. Radar was also helping. Radar was new during the war, and it was secret.

At night, suppose you throw a ball into the dark. If the ball springs back at you, it has hit something. Something is there in the dark. Radar threw radio signals into the night sky. When the signals hit a plane, they were thrown back again. In this way, radar found enemy planes in the dark.

In the radar station, the signals were shown as points of light. A radar officer watched a dark 'picture' of the sky. A plane very close to the station caused a bright point near the middle of the picture. The places of the signal told the radar officer where the plane was—left or right, in front or behind. It's not surprising that radars were soon seeing UFOs.

One morning in September of 1951, a number of Air Force officers were visiting a radar school in New Jersey, and a student was showing how radar worked. For a time they watched the points of light moving across the picture— planes in the area.

Then the student noticed the signal from an object 1000 metres away, and flying low. He couldn't identify it. 'It's going too fast for a jet,' he said. There was surprise among the visitors—what could go faster than a jet? They watched it for three minutes, then it left the picture.

At 3.15 the same afternoon the radar showed something else, at the same place where the earlier object left the picture. This one was travelling slowly—but 28,000 metres high—and what could fly as high as 28 km? Next morning, *two* radars found an object that flew very fast up into the sky, and down again. And that afternoon, another object that travelled slowly for several minutes. Like the others, no one could identify it.

There have been many radar UFOs since then. And to understand most of them, you need to understand something about radar itself. The sender of radar signals turns slowly round and round all the time. Suppose you're sitting on top of a post 8 km high, and the post is slowly turning. You can't see all round you, only in front of you (like through a telescope).

Suppose now that you see a plane. You know something is there, and you know how far away. But you can't stop turning, so you lose the plane almost at once. A few seconds later perhaps, you've turned all the way round. The plane is still there, but it's not quite in the same place. It has moved of course. But again you lose it, and you must wait a few seconds before you see it again.

A radar works in the same kind of way. It doesn't follow an object all the time: it sees the object once in every turn. Suppose the radar 'sees' a balloon. And as the sender is turning, the balloon breaks into thousands of pieces that fall to the ground. When the radar points towards the balloon's place again, there's nothing there. The radar officer, of course, hasn't seen a balloon: all he has seen is a point of light in a dark picture. One second it was there, then—nothing.

The early radar people always thought of 'flying objects'. This one has clearly flown over the skyline. Many kilometres in only a second or two. Too high a speed for a plane

—so it must be a UFO, from some other planet.

And when a signal is lost, it doesn't always mean the object has broken up. If a plane flies too low, radar can lose it. And a difference of a few metres can cause this kind of trouble.

The radar picture

A radar doesn't give you a 'picture' like a camera, of course: only a number of bright points. And each point of light tells you: something has thrown back the radar signals. Nothing more. It doesn't tell you *what* the signals have hit.

And you don't always know where the signals have travelled since they were sent. When you send out light, some of it may hit a number of shiny objects before it comes back to you. Certain objects are 'shiny' to radar signals, and can give you some strange surprises. These objects may be large trucks, buildings, small hills.

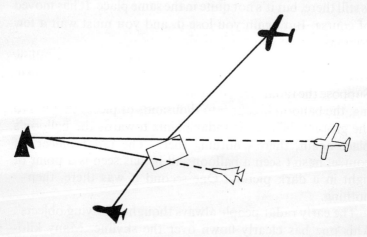

Fig. 29 Will the two white 'planes' crash?

When more than one plane comes into the picture, you can sometimes get a number of UFOs. In Fig. 31, the radar officer will receive two signals—but both in the wrong place. As the two planes move, the two points of light may come together. On radar, it can look like a plane crash. But when a pilot reports that nothing is wrong, the radar officer may think something different has happened: a UFO flew very fast towards a plane, then just missed it.

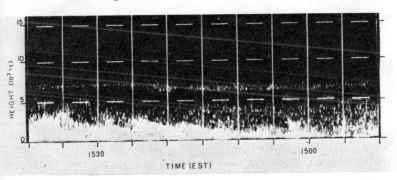

Fig. 30

And planes of course are not the only objects that fly. In fig. 30, the signals near the ground are caused by flies and other insects. There are so many small light-points at the bottom of the picture that the paper there is almost white.

Other signals are caused by birds. Even drops of water show up as signals, and for that reason radars are used to look for rain. Radio signals can cause radar UFOs, and there are many radio signals in the air these days—not only from radios themselves, but from television, cars, airports.

But perhaps most radar UFOs have been caused by the air itself. Usually the air becomes colder and drier as you go higher up. But there are times when the higher air is less cold or less dry. Air in this state can do strange things to radar signals.

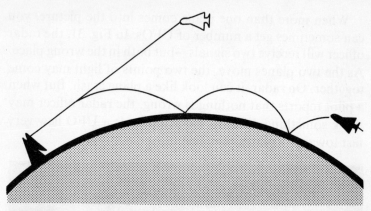

Fig. 31

It can cause radar to bend down to the ground—then perhaps up and down again a number of times. A radar officer can think he's looking at a signal from high in the sky, but it may be from a house or a car on the ground. And since the air is always moving like a sea, it can pull radar about in unusual ways.

A signal may hit a truck in one place, then almost at once, something else many kilometres away. At the radar station, it can seem that some object has moved very fast from one place to another.

Usually a radar station can't 'see' for many kilometres. But when the signals are thrown down to the ground and up and down again, it can sometimes 'see' for thousands of kilometres. And the radar officer doesn't always know when this is happening.

During the war, a ship in the Mediterranean Sea saw an enemy ship on its radar, and fired at it. It reported that the enemy was sunk. That 'enemy ship' was Malta—many kilometres away. Those guns were firing at a radar signal, and Malta is happily still above water.

At sea near Japan in 1944, American ships reported a new

and fearful enemy during the hours of night. 'Something' kept coming towards them at a high speed. Just before the object crashed into a ship, the radar lost it. The air can throw back radar signals that look like a number of fast UFOs.

In the early days of radar, many of the signals were not understood, and radar itself had a number of problems. Radar today is very different from those first few years. And as radar became better, UFOs became fewer.

Every place has its own radar surprises. And when a radar officer moves to a new station, he must learn about them. We also know now that *one* unknown in a radar picture is almost useless to us. There are so many possible causes, it's no good trying to find the answer to one unknown.

Radar today can get a signal from one fly at a distance of 20 km—and there are rather a lot of flies about. We know that even clear air can send signals back to a radar station.

The big radars at Wallops Island, in Virginia, have spent five years studying these signals. In these studies, the causes of *all* the unusual signals were understood. Some signals came from near the ground, and the air bent them. Some were insects. Some were birds. And some were sent back by changes in the air itself. There were no unknowns, and no UFOs at all.

Twenty or thirty years ago, we just didn't know enough about radar—and *that* was the cause of radar UFOs.

The secret of the Foo Fighters

In 1956 a Royal Canadian Air Force pilot, was flying a jet fighter above the Rocky Mountains, 11 km up. And he watched a shining UFO for about 45 seconds: he thought it was about 15 to 30 metres across, but it's hard to be sure about this.

A shining ball of air like this is a *plasma*. Some kinds of plasmas have been known for many years: others are new to us. The reasons for them are not well known, and their cause is not understood.

In 1956 a plane was flying over Russia when the pilot saw a red ball of fire shooting towards him. It was about 30 cm across. It hit near the front of the plane in a great white light, and a long line of fire ran along the plane's left side. The bang was heard above the sound of the engine. But the plane was unhurt.

And when a big red 'ball of fire' hit the front of an American plane in 1952, the pilot thought he'd crashed into another plane. But again the plane was unhurt: no one could find a hole or even a mark.

During the war, some pilots saw shining balls of fire shooting towards them, or following them. These strange objects were named Foo Fighters, but they never seemed to hurt anyone. After the war, everyone learned that these were not secret enemy flying-objects—*both* sides met them.

On the ground, plasmas have been reported for many years. People have said that a plasma looks like a hard object, and not something 'made of air'. It often shines brightly, and no one can see through it. The air inside it moves, and the plasma seems to be turning round and round. Usually the ball seems to be 'burning'.

Plasma-UFOs

You can get plasmas on high-power electric lines. They can happen when something goes wrong, and too much electricity passes along the power lines. Dirt on the lines can help to cause plasmas, and so can insects. Plasmas also change colour as their electrical power changes.

A plasma is electrical, and there are two kinds of electricity. Two *like* kinds push each other away, and two *unlike* kinds will come together. A pilot sometimes reports that a UFO seems to stay at the same distance from him. When he flies towards it, it moves away. When he turns, it turns. If a plane moves away, the UFO seems to wait. And when the plane returns and gets closer, the UFO moves away again.

It often seems that 'somebody' is in charge of UFOs like these. But these moves are not surprising if the plane shows largely the same kind of electricity as the plasma. People and cars can push plasmas away or pull them closer for the same reasons.

And if a UFO is a plasma, it's easy for it to move one way, stop, and move at once another way, even at high speeds. Electric signals shoot across your TV picture, from left to right and back again, thousands of times a second.

And plasmas will not only send back radar signals: the signals from plasma can be *stronger* than signals from something hard. When a satellite returns from the moon, it hits the air at high speed. The air around it becomes a plasma, and no one can talk to the men in the satellite by radio—the plasma throws back the signals.

Plasmas don't usually last very long, and when they break up, there's nothing left to see. So a plasma can show a strong signal on the radar picture, and then—nothing. Another UFO has clearly 'flown over the skyline'—at thousands of kilometres an hour.

But in 1966, in North Carolina, A F Jenzano wasn't just identifying plasma-UFOs—he was *making* them. 'What form would you like?' he said. 'You name it and we'll make it. Saucer? Pencil? Ball? What colour would you like—red, blue, green?'

Jenzano begins with a glass case with round sides. He takes away most of the air, then he fires high-power electricity inside the glass case. He can get different kinds of plasma when he uses less or more air or electricity.

Since then, other people have made plasmas. The parts with less electricity are darker. With a UFO like this at a distance, for a few seconds, it's easy to 'see' holes, windows, people.

Space-visitors in the past?

So do we have visitors from space? No one has brought forward any reasons for believing it. But sometimes the question had been changed: Have we *had* visitors from space? Did they come here hundreds, perhaps thousands, of years ago? How can we know?

The answers to this question are usually like this: 'Some of the people in this old painting are dressed *like* spacemen.' 'These round objects in the sky in this old drawing—they *could* be UFOs.' 'The "rings of fire" in this old story—they *may* be spaceships.'

But there are many other ways to explain the same things. Unhappily no one can make a clear story out of *could* and *may* and *if* and *perhaps*.

As Carl Sagan has said, there are only two kinds of thing that we could believe: an *object*, or *something written*. A 10-thousand-year-old piece from a television or a satellite-engine would be fine. Or a very old drawing of part of a radio. Or some numbers that told us the distances of our planets from the sun, or the speed of light.

But nothing like this of course has ever been found. Even from the thousands of reported UFOs of the last few years, nothing has been found. No UFO has ever crashed, or even been in trouble. No one has ever discovered the smallest part of one.

There have been reports of course. But the pieces have

always been from objects made on this planet, and have shown nothing unusual.

So UFOs have given nothing *to* us: but have they taken anything *from* us?

Is somebody stealing ships?

If something is lost, has a UFO stolen it?

If you draw a line from Bermuda to Florida to Puerto Rico, and back again to Bermuda, you will have an area of water in the form of a triangle—the Bermuda Triangle. Several ships have been lost in the Bermuda Triangle.

The usual story is that a ship travels into the Triangle on a clear, fine day. Its radio signals give no sign of trouble. And then—the ship isn't there any more.

The truth is that none of this has anything to do with UFOs: nobody saw any unidentified flying objects at any time. But now that UFOs are becoming fewer and fewer, believers are having to find signs of them in strange places.

But it isn't very unusual for ships to be lost at sea. It would be much easier to 'steal' one of our satellites. But none of the hundreds of satellites has ever been missing.

There was a big meeting about UFOs, in Boston, in 1969. And Professor Philip Morrison asked an interesting question: 'How many *trains* have been lost?' None. If something goes wrong, a train is easy to find. But if something goes wrong with a ship, it's often hard to find—because it's under thousands of metres of water.

We don't need UFOs to understand missing ships and planes.

Reporting the impossible

If there are no visitors from space, why do we still sometimes get UFO reports?

Most UFO reports come from people who can't report clearly what they see. The reports themselves often tell of the impossible.

There are a number of reports of UFOs that travel at high speeds: sometimes thousands of kilometres an hour. Nearly all these reports say there was 'no sound'. A report like this is just wrong. It's impossible to travel through the air at more than 1500 kph without making a sound. When a plane passes you at faster than the speed of sound, it makes two large bangs. (They may sound like one, but it's still a big bang.) And *any* faster-than-sound object will make this bang. It doesn't matter if the object is from this planet or another. This kind of report has to be wrong.

Other people have said that a UFO stopped their car engine electrically. It's certainly possible to make a car engine useless, if you use electricity that's powerful enough. But after the UFO passed, the car engine was always all right, and the owner drove off again.

But stories of engine trouble have been told before. In England near the beginning of the war, people near the new secret radar-stations said the same thing. They didn't know what radar was, and they didn't know what was happening in a radar station. But sometimes when they drove their cars past this new and strange place, the engine stopped. When people knew what radar was, their car engines didn't seem to stop any more. But it was not the radar that changed —it was the people.

Sometimes we know the true cause of a UFO. Then it's interesting to look at people's reports. One night in 1967, there was a report of a UFO 23 metres long and 6 metres across. There were about 'twelve lights' under it, and they were brighter than a car's headlights.

This UFO was a bag, no more than one metre long. A

young boy placed six small candles under the open mouth. He lit the candles, and sent up his hot-air balloon into the night.

The next year, two boys made the same kind of hot-air balloon, and sent it up near Denver. A UFO was reported with 'a big bright light'. It was about '180 m high and 8 m across'. And it 'shot up into the sky, throwing out balls of fire'.

There are many small pieces of matter flying through space, and sometimes they reach us and fall to the ground. A bright one is a fireball, and several fireballs have become UFOs.

Professor Frank Drake talked with many people who saw them. He says, 'About 14 per cent report a loud sound when they saw a fireball. Even if there *is* a sound, how could it reach them as fast as light? And people at different distances report the sound at the same time. It just isn't possible.'

It seems that a loud sound 'goes with' a bright light in many people's minds.

Drake also found that people didn't remember things for long. 'After one day, about half the reports are clearly wrong. After two days, about 75 per cent are clearly wrong. After four days only 10 per cent are good. After five days, there is little truth left. UFO teams usually ask their questions days after the happening. It's not much use.'

When the time on a clock seems to be impossible, you don't think that time itself has gone wrong. It's not time that's gone wrong—it's the clock. And it's the clock that you study. In the same way, when a man tells you something that seems impossible, study the man.

Carl Sagan says: 'I don't mind when people can't identify UFOs. It's when some of these people identify them—that's when the trouble starts.'

Zond Four

As you get more and more reports about something (says the Condon Report), you ought to learn more and more about it. But not with UFOs. As you get more and more reports of a UFO, you know less and less about it. More reports bring more differences.

One of the most surprising UFOs was seen, not by a few people, but by hundreds. And not only in one place, but in different parts of the USA—Indiana, Kentucky, Massachusetts, New York, Ohio, Pennsylvania, Tennessee, Virginia, and West Virginia. Hundreds of people saw bright objects flying across the sky, and shooting out a rain of fire.

At about 8.45 on the evening of March 3, 1968, three people looked up at the night sky. One of them later reported: 'A light was travelling across the sky. Rather larger than a star, and about the same colour. It came towards us, then flew above us. It was in the form of a fat pencil. About as big as one of our largest planes, and it had windows. These windows were lit up, and the light from them was quite bright. A long line of red fire was shooting out at the back. There was no sound. It was less than about 300 metres above the ground.'

A schoolteacher from Ohio watched it through field-glasses. She began her report: 'This is certainly a UFO'. As it got nearer to the skyline, she said, the object became three. The colours were red and white. Her own ears could make out no sound, but her dog became afraid, and went and hid. She signalled to the object with a torch, but she got no answer.

'Something made me very sleepy,' she said. 'It was a powerful feeling, and I had to fight it. I tried hard to stay awake. This was unusual for me. The same thing once happened to me before, when I saw a UFO in 1966.'

A report from Indiana said, 'The object flew no higher than the tree tops. We saw it very clearly, because it was only a few metres away. It was like a long jet plane, with many windows. It was on fire in front and behind.'

A car driver said the object turned and changed course. That night, hundreds of people telephoned airports and police stations.

Few people report just what they see. If a man sees three bright points moving across the sky, he doesn't usually say, 'I saw three bright points moving across the sky.' He may say, 'I saw three *lights*.' He may report, 'There were three lights *flying* across the sky.'

Someone else may think that the lights were *held together*. Another may talk about *an object with three lights on it*. He may think he *saw* the object that held the lights. And the report becomes: 'It was a dark object...something like a pencil...with lights—windows...flying across the sky... at high speed.' All this has grown from *three bright points moving across the sky*.

And this happened with many of the reports on that evening in March 1968.

One man 'heard' a sound. Others said the 'object' was in the form of a saucer. Some reported that it had 'clear edges'. One person said there was more than one object: one was 'trying to catch another, and shoot it down'. Some said it was perhaps 30 km above the ground: others thought it was only a few metres up. And the lights were reported as 'red and blue'.

The cause of this UFO was Zond Four, a Russian satellite. Something went wrong, and Zond Four came down. When it reached the air, it became hot, and broke into pieces—the bright points in the sky. It was then more than 120 km above the ground.

For this UFO, we have the true cause and the reports.

For some UFOs, we have only the reports. The break-up of Zond Four has something interesting to teach us: a report itself is just not enough.

How to use Father Christmas

If a spaceship does reach us from another planet, it has travelled millions of kilometres. And the journey has taken hundreds, thousands, perhaps millions of years. If even one spaceship reaches us, this will be unusual. It's surely not possible for hundreds of them to get here every year.

We can talk about the possible speed of a spaceship, and the distance of its journey, and the time it takes, and the kind of engine it may have, and so on. But there are many things here that we don't know. There's a better way to study this whole question.

Carl Sagan says, try it with the story of Father Christmas. There's a story that every year on December 25 (Christmas Day) Father Christmas brings presents to every home. He travels all through the night of December 24, and his presents are pulled through the sky by animals. Is this story true?

We could (says Sagan) talk about the animals, and their speed, and how they can fly, where Father Christmas comes from—and so on. But there's an easier way.

Just look at the numbers. Suppose Father Christmas is at each house for only one second. And suppose he needs no time at all to go from one house to another. In the USA he must visit a hundred million houses. So he takes a hundred million seconds—that's three years. And three years just won't go into one night. So the story is untrue.

Now, says Sagan, look at the story of UFOs in the same way. Suppose there are one-million planets that can send out spaceships*. There are surely 10-thousand-million interesting places to visit, and our world is one of them. And suppose that only one spaceship comes to us every year.

This means that every planet with spaceships is sending out 10-thousand of them each year. And 27 spaceships every day is just too much to believe.

The American Hong-Yee Chiu has tried a different line of thought.

'A spaceship,' he says, 'could be no smaller than an Apollo satellite.'

How much matter is needed for all these spaceships? Hong-Yee Chiu has found out: they would need the matter from half-a-million stars. Again, it's impossible to believe the spaceship story.

There are other questions with no good answers. If the UFO reports are true, the hundreds or thousands of spaceships are nearly all different. They have different forms, different numbers of legs, they move in different ways, each 'pilot' must fly a different spaceship in a different way. Why? It would be a great waste of time and money and trouble.

Reports often say that UFOs come close to planes in flight, and 'study' them. The best place for this would be above an airport—there are plenty of planes there. But UFOs are almost never reported over busy airports. Why not?

If UFOs do want to look at our planes, they can do it best in daylight. But usually they seem to do their studying at night. Why?

And why planes? If a spaceship can travel for perhaps thousands of years through space, what's interesting about a plane?

* "Is Anybody There?" (Books in Easy English)

Identified Flying Objects

What about the men in our own satellites? Why don't they see flying saucers? They sometimes see things they don't understand. But they don't at once talk about spaceships from other planets.

James McDivitt saw something when he was in the satellite Gemini Four. When he was asked about it, he said, 'I did see something; and some people would call it a UFO. But remember that UFO just means Unidentified Flying Object. The object I saw is still unidentified. This does not mean it was a spaceship from another planet. And it doesn't mean that it wasn't. It only means that I saw something, and I couldn't identify it.'

Reports as careful as this are unusual!

There are now large numbers of objects in the space round our planet. In the ten years up to 1967, we sent up 2606 objects. And at the end of that time, 1139 of them were still up there.

Suppose a spaceship is 30 metres across. The big American telescope at Palomar could still see it 80 kilometres away.

And there are now radar stations watching the skies day and night for enemies. American and Russian satellites sometimes break up into hundreds of very small pieces. The radars find them and follow them.

It's impossible for the radars to miss a spaceship of any kind. *People* have often reported spaceships. But spaceships have never been reported by the big radars. And the radars watch day and night, and they can find a lost ball as far away as the moon!

The two questions

Isaac Asimov has perhaps written more space stories than anyone. 'Space travel,' he says, 'needs spaceships with very great power. If anyone pilots a ship all the way across deep space, he won't waste any time and power when he gets here. He won't fly about here for years, doing nothing, wasting power. If they *want* to meet us, they *will* meet us. If not, they'll save their power, and go away.'

It's not enough to believe that a UFO report is true. *You must be able to show other people that it's true*. No one has ever done this.

A UFO report, says Carl Sagan, must answer *two questions*:   (1) Is it *interesting*?   (2) Must I *believe it*? And the answer to both questions must be *yes*.

'Suppose,' he says, 'we are talking about little green men. Suppose 500 different holiday-makers see something green —not very clearly—in the forest. That's 500 different reports—surely I ought to *believe* them. But—an unclear green thing? It may be only a bird. Not *interesting*. Now suppose one man is walking through the forest. He says he saw 7000 little green men. And they took him down a hole in the ground, and showed him their gold and their little green hats. I will say, "Great! Who else went along?" And he will say, "Nobody." Or "A friend." Now this report is *interesting*, but I don't have to *believe* it. I want the 500 holiday-makers to find the 7000 little green men. It's the same thing with UFOs. The reports I can *believe* are not *interesting*. And the *interesting* reports are ones I can't *believe*. Unhappily no reports are both interesting *and* make me believe them.'

No one has ever answered yes to the two questions.

Suppose you do see a UFO? What then? Arthur C Clarke has a few words of help for you:

'It's not a spaceship until you can read the Mars number. But if you keep looking at the sky, one day you *will* see a true spaceship. It will be one of ours.'

Some words and their meanings

The **Air Force** is in charge of a government's planes
An **airport** is a landing-place for air travellers
A **balloon** is a large bag filled with hot air
When something is **bright**, it shines
You take photographs with a **camera**
A **candle** gives light
Christmas (December 25) is a holiday, and people give presents
When planes **crash**, they hit the ground and break up
What is its **distance**? = How far away is it?
We use **electric** power for light, radio, Tv
The **engine** makes the power that drives a car or plane
Field glasses you look through field glasses to see distant objects
In a camera, the pictures are formed on the **film**
When you name something, you **identify** it
A fly is one kind of **insect**
You watch a **movie** in the cinema
An **object** is anything you could touch
Oxygen is in the air: your body needs it all the time
A **photograph** is the picture that a camera makes
A **pilot** flies planes
A **planet** is a world that moves round a sun
Plasma—see page 53 and 54
Radar—see page 46
Powerfully **radio-active** things can slowly kill you if you stand too close
Tell me what happened = Give me a **report**
A **satellite** travels round the world, above the air
A **saucer** rests under a cup
If something is **secret**, you must not tell it to anyone
Planes can talk to other planes by radio **signals**
When you have travelled away from the world and its air, you are in **space**
What is its **speed**? = How fast is it?
The shining points of light in the night sky are **stars**
You look through a **telescope** with one eye to see the stars clearly
A **triangle** is a form with three sides